CHAMELEONS
AND AGAMIDS...

ERIK D. STOOPS

Faulkner's Publishing Group

This book is dedicated to Dan Faulkner. Thank you for all your help.

Library of Congress Catalog Card Number 97-60517.

COVER PHOTO: Chinese Water Dragon by Bill LuBack's Reptiles
DESIGNED BY: Graphic Arts & Production, Inc., Plover, WI

Faulkner's Publishing Group
200 Paw Paw Ave. #124
Benton Harbor, MI 49022

©1997 by Erik Daniel Stoops
Faulkner's ISBN 1-890475-03-3 Lib

Table of Contents

Chapter One

What are Chameleons and Agamids?

How many species of Chameleons and Agamids are there?

What is a Frilled Dragon?

Read on to learn all about Chameleons and Agamids.

What is a Chameleon?

Chameleons are a group of lizards that belong to the family Chameleonidae (Kuh-mee-lee-on-oh-dee). They are very easy to recognize. Some species have three horns or a crest on top of their head, others have the ability to change many different colors. Its body is flattened on both sides. Chameleons have large eyes which can be moved independently of each other. The word Chameleon comes from the Greek word, Chamaele, which means little lion.

CHINESE WATER DRAGON ▲

What is an Agamid?

Agamids are a group of lizards that are closely related to the Iguanid lizard group. They are different than other species of lizards because they have different aspects in their general biology Agamid (A-gam-id). Common characteristics of Agamids are thin tails, long legs and plump bodies. Agamids have many famous lizards in their family such as the Frilled Dragon.

by Pat Turcott

◀ THE CHAMELEON HAS THE ABILITY TO CHANGE MANY DIFFERENT COLORS IN ORDER TO BLEND IN WITH THEIR SURROUNDINGS. WHEN CHAMELEONS ARE ANGRY, THEY MAY CHANGE TO COLORS SUCH AS BLACK AND YELLOW TO WARN OFF THEIR ENEMIES.

Are Chameleons and Agamids cold-blooded or warm-blooded?

All species of lizards are **cold-blooded**. They need the warm sun during the day to help them move and digest their food.

How many species of Chameleons and Agamids are there?

Chameleons consist of 85 species. The Agamids, according to *scientists*, consist of about 300 species.

Are lizards related to dinosaurs?

According to *herpetologists* and scientists, many species of reptiles, including lizards, were thought to be related to the dinosaurs. This is still up for debate. *Paleontologists* have found that the dinosaurs were more closely related to the birds.

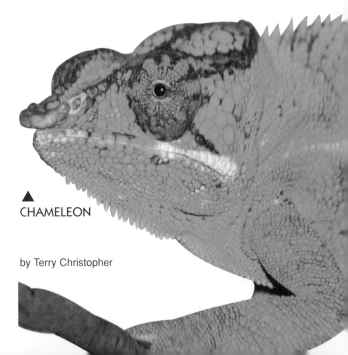
▲ CHAMELEON

by Terry Christopher

6

CHAMELEONS AND AGAMIDS

Frilled Dragon:

This is one of Australia's most popular lizard species. They are known for their impressive frill which looks like a hood on their neck. They are also known for running on their hind legs. They can reach up to 1 to 3 feet in length. They feed on insects and small mammals.

◄ THE FRILLED DRAGON LOOKS LIKE IT HAS AN UMBRELLA ON ITS HEAD, WHICH IS ACTUALLY LARGE FOLDS OF SKIN THAT HELP THE LIZARD WARN OFF ENEMIES.

y Bill LuBack's Reptiles

IF YOU LOOK CLOSELY, YOU CAN SEE ► A LARGE BEARD OF SPINES ON THE NECK OF THIS BEARDED DRAGON.

Bearded Dragon:

This lizard is best known for having a beard formed by a arge fold at the chin, covered with sharp spines. They re found in Australia and feed on small insects and nammals. They can reach up to 12 inches in length.

by Pat Turcott

7

Thorny Devil (Moloch):

This is Australia's weirdest lizard species. Its body and tail are covered with large spiny scales. They have a strange pattern of yellow, red and brown. They live in the deserts and plains of Central and Southern Australia and can grow up to 6 inches long. They lay 6-8 eggs.

Flying Dragon (Draco):

The Draco, as it is known, is found in the Philippines and Malaysia. There are 16 species of Dracos. They are best known for having loose flaps of scaly skin which they use to glide from branch to branch. They feed on small insects and can grow to 8 1/2 inches.

◄ THE FLYING DRAGON LOOKS LIKE A REPTILIAN BUTTERFLY WITH BRILLIANT COLORS ON ITS WINGS.

by Wai Lui

Jackson's Chameleon:

This is one of the largest species of Chameleons which is found in Africa. Their ability to change color is highly developed. The Jackson's Chameleon is known for having horns on its head. Males have three large horns. Females have only one small horn on their head and two smaller undeveloped horns near their eyes. Females lay large amounts of eggs. They mainly feed on insects and can reach lengths of almost 5 inches.

THIS JACKSON'S CHAMELEON IS A MALE. YOU CAN TELL THIS BY THE THREE HORNS ON HIS HEAD. THEY CAN CATCH FLIES AND CRICKETS WITH THEIR LONG, STICKY TONGUE.

▼

by Pat Turcott

Chapter Two

Where are Chameleons and Agamids Found?

Where do Agamids live?

Can lizards climb trees?

Read on to find the answers to these questions and more.

Where do Agamids live?

Agamids can be found in Africa, central, south and southeast Australia, and one species can be found in Europe. They live in climates such as deserts, rocky canyons and rain forests.

Where do Chameleons live?

Chameleons can be found in Africa, Madagascar, south Asia and southern Europe. They are mostly a rain forest species because they enjoy high humidity. There is one species, the Yeman Chameleon, that makes its home in a desert of Africa.

Where is the best place to find a lizard?

If I were a lizard, this is where I would be:

- Under a rock
- On a rock
- In a field
- On a house
- In a tree
- In a rain forest

by Terry Odegaard

▲ MANY SPECIES OF LIZARDS MAKE THEIR HOMES IN LARGE TREES LIKE THIS ONE.

Can lizards swim?

Some species of Agamids are great swimmers, such as the Water Dragon. They use their legs and tail to help them glide in the water. Chameleons are not good swimmers at all.

Can lizards climb trees?

Yes. The Chameleons of the Africa/ Madagascar desert spend much of their lives in trees and are found to be wonderful climbers.

Chapter Three

Senses

Can lizards see colors?

Do lizards have tongues and what are they used for?

Read on and see if you can find the answers
to these questions and more.

by Wai Lui

by Pat Turcott

Do Chameleons and Agamids sleep?

Yes. Some species of Agamids sleep at night, such as the Frilled Lizard. Chameleons sleep during the day and are active all night long.

Do lizards have tongues and what are they used for?

Lizards use their tongues for many different things. They use them to smell, taste, feel the vibrations in the air and on the ground, as well as to eat with. A Chameleon can use its tongue to catch insects. Their tongue can be as long as their entire body.

Do Chameleons and Agamids have ears?

Yes. Lizard's ears, which are two tiny holes, are located near the eyes. They hear vibrations in the air which help them find food and stay safe from their enemies.

What exactly do lizards see?

The Chameleon has excellent eyesight which allows it to see its prey much better. Lizards can see up close, but most species rely on their other senses to get them through the day and night.

Can lizards see colors?

Scientists have found that certain species of lizards can see colors such as red and yellow. Many scientists are still learning about this spectacular finding.

Do lizards have eyelids?

Yes. Unlike snakes, all species of lizards have eyelids. Like our eyelids, they protect the lizard's eyes from dirt and predators.

◀ BABY WATER DRAGON

by Pat Turcott

15

Chapter Four

Eating Habits

How do Chameleons capture their food?

Do lizards have teeth?

Read on to find these answers and more.

by Terry Christopher

▲
THIS PANTHER CHAMELEON USES ITS LONG, STICKY TONGUE
TO CAPTURE ITS DINNER.

How do Chameleons capture their food?

Lizards use their eyesight and their strong sense of smell to find their food. Chameleons shoot their tongue out of their mouth almost a full bodies length in order to catch their prey. At the end of their tongue is a sticky pad to which the prey adheres to.

What do Chameleons and Agamids eat?

Lizards eat many different things such as mammals, reptiles, insects, fish and snails. Each species has its own type of food it eats. For example, the Chameleon likes to eat insects, while Agamids will eat a wide variety of foods such as insects, small lizards and vegetation.

Do lizards get fat?

In captivity, Agamid species that do not get very much exercise often become overweight. This is not healthy for lizards and can cause diseases.

17

Do Chameleons and Agamids chew their food?

No. They swallow their food whole. They use their teeth for tearing chunks off and then swallow. Some lizards have very small teeth and may use their tongue to help them tear chunks off before swallowing.

Do lizards have teeth?

Yes. Many species have teeth to grasp onto food items. Their teeth are also used to help the lizards swallow their food.

FEMALE CHAMAELEO CALYPTRATUS ▶

How often do Chameleons and Agamids eat?

Chameleons in captivity will eat almost every day, while in the wild, many species may only eat every two or three days.

by Wai Lui

18

Do lizards throw up?

When a lizard is sick or has eaten something that doesn't agree with it, it often throws up. This is sometimes harmful to the lizard because they tend to become dehydrated when this happens.

by Pat Turcott

Do Chameleons and Agamids drink?

Yes. All species of lizards need to drink water to survive. They often do this by lapping the dewdrops off leaves and plants, sometimes off themselves after a rain.

THIS SPECIES
NAME IS
GONIOCEPHALUS
GRANDIS. ▶

by Wai Lui

Chapter Five

Lizard Reproduction

How do lizards give birth?

How do you tell the difference between male and female lizards?

Read on to answer these questions and more.

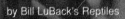

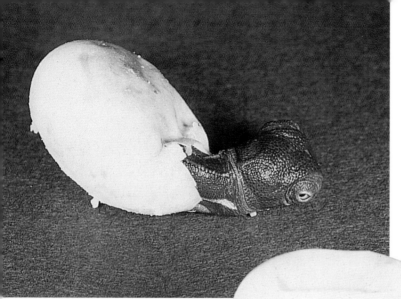

◀ CHAMELEON HATCHING

by Wai Lui

THIS BABY CHAMELEON IS NOW
READY TO FACE THE WORLD.
▼

by Wai Lui

When do Chameleons and Agamids mate?

They may often seek a mate during the rainy season or spring in their geographic location.

How do lizards lay eggs?

Lizards lay eggs through their *anal plate*. Some lizards can lay up to 30 eggs. As an egg-laying species, the Bearded Dragon often will bury her eggs in a safe, warm, moist place.

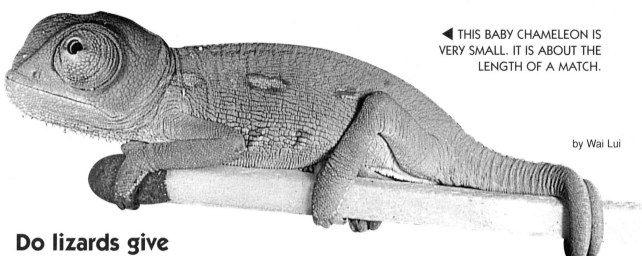

by Wai Lui

Do lizards give live birth?

Yes. They give birth the same way as egg-laying species, through the anal plate. The *neonates,* "newborns," will often be born in an egg yolk placenta sack which they usually break out of when born. Baby lizards use their egg tooth to do this. The egg tooth usually falls off in about a week. Sometimes the exhausted mother lizard will eat the placenta sack for nutrition.

Will male lizards fight for the female?

Yes. Males will often court potential females and may often show signs of display to impress the female. Male iguanas may often fight one another for the right to mate. The fight might look bad, but it is usually not fatal.

How do you tell the difference between male and female?

In some species of lizards, males may be more colorful or larger than the female. In other species, such as geckos, males may have larger tails than females. Male lizards have hemi-penes located in the anal plate which is used for mating.

Chapter Six

Self-Defense

How do lizards protect themselves?

Can Chameleons or Agamids lose their tail?

Read on to learn all about Chameleons
and Agamids ways of self-defense.

Why do Chameleons and Agamids have scales?

Chameleons have smooth scales which are used to keep them on their toes through camouflage, while Agamids such as the common African Agama have rough scales. These are used for protection against their enemies.

by Bill LuBack's Reptiles

▲
FRILLED DRAGON

Can a Chameleon or an Agamid lose their tail?

Yes. Some species of Agamids can lose their tail when they are frightened, or in order to get away from predators. The tail often grows back within a few months.

What does endangered species mean?

The word **endangered** means a species threatened with extinction. Every day a number of species of animals becomes endangered or even extinct.

How do lizards protect themselves?

Some species, such as the Frilled Dragon, will often spread the hood on its neck to scare off its enemies. Others, like the Chameleon, will hiss and open its mouth. Chameleons will change color to blend in with their surroundings in order to hide from their enemies.

What can I do to protect lizards?

The best thing to do to protect lizards, besides just leaving them alone, is to pick up litter and throw it in a garbage receptacle. You should learn more about the lizards in your area so you can help protect them. It is very rewarding when you do this and makes you feel good.

25

Chapter Seven

Facts about Chameleons and Agamids

What do lizards die from?

How do their muscles work?

Read on to learn many interesting facts about
Chameleons and Agamids.

by Bill LuBack's Reptiles

A PAIR OF FRILLED DRAGONS ▲

What do lizards die from?

Many lizards die from diseases such as *viruses* and bacteria which they can catch from other lizards. Lizards can catch colds, cough and sneeze like we do. They also die of stress due to being held in captivity. They can die from *parasites* that crawl on their body and some that live in their body. *Poachers* may often kill lizards for their skin or catch them to sell to people. This is not very fair to the lizards.

If I want to see a lizard, where should I look?

The safest place to see a lizard is at a zoo. Many zoos have several kinds of species on display from all over the world. It is best not to catch lizards from the wild and keep them in your home. Leave them where they belong.

27

by Pat Turcott

JACKSON'S CHAMELEON ▲

How do their muscles work?

Some species of Agamids have strong, powerful muscles that help them move on the ground. Chameleons have strong, flexible muscles that help them climb and move in trees and bushes.

If I want to be a scientist and study lizards, what will I be?

If you want to study lizards when you grow up you can become a *herpetologist*. Many herpetologists spend their whole lives trying to protect and conserve different species of lizards.

How do scientists classify lizards?

Scientists, called taxonomists, help to identify and name animals. The names that are given to lizards sometimes tell what color they are or where they are from. Lizards have two names that are easy to remember, but change from country to country. The scientific names that are mostly used by scientists do not change very often. A common name for the Frilled Lizard is Frilled Dragon, but the scientific name is *Chlamydosaurus King II*.

Let's classify a Chameleon:

The *family* of Chameleon is Chamelonidae.

A *species* of Chameleon is a
Parsons Chameleon.

Let's classify an Agamid:

The *family* of Agamid
is Agamidae.

A *species* of
Agamidae
is a Frilled
Dragon.

by Wai Lui

Glossary

Anal Plate:
The large scale between the back legs of the lizard.

Chlamydosaurus King II:
A scientific name for frilled lizard.

Cold-Blooded:
Having a body temperature not internally regulated, but approximately that of the environment.

Endangered: Threatened with extinction.

Endemic:
Native to a particular country, nation or region.

External:
Having merely the outward appearance of something.

Fossil:
A remnant impression, or trace of an animal or plant of past geological ages that has been preserved in the earth's crust.

Herpetologist:
One who studies reptiles and amphibians.

Neonate: Newborn.

Paleontologist:
One who studies the science dealing with the life of past geological periods as known from fossil remains.

Parasite:
An organism that lives in or on another organism at whose expense it receives nourishment.

Poacher:
One who kills or takes game and fish illegally.

Quadrupole:
A system composed of two dipoles of equal but oppositely directed moment.

Rhynchocephalian:
A class of reptile.

Scientist:
A scientific investigator.

Unisexual:
All individuals are females that can lay eggs and are fertile without mating.

Virus:
The causative agent of an infectious disease.

Warm-Blooded:
Having a relatively high and constant body temperature relatively independent of the surroundings.

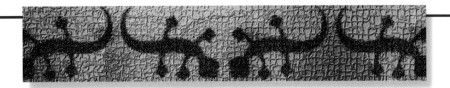

Books and CD-Roms Written by the Author Suggested Reading

Snakes and Other Reptiles of the Southwest

Erik D. Stoops & Annette T. Wright. 1991. Golden West Publishing Company, Phoenix, Arizona. Scientific Field Guide.

Snakes

Erik D. Stoops & Annette T. Wright. 1992. Hardback and Paperback. Sterling Publishing Company, New York. Children's non-fiction, full-color, question and answer format. First Book in Children's Nature Library Series.

Breeding Boas and Pythons

Erik D. Stoops & Annette T. Wright. 1993. TFH Publishing Company, New York. Scientific Care and Breeding Guide.

Sharks

Erik D. Stoops & Sherrie L. Stoops. Illustrated by Jeffrey L. Martin. June, 1994. Hardback and Paperback. Sterling Publishing Company, New York. Children's non-fiction, full-color, question and answer format. Second Book in Children's Nature Library Series.

Dolphins

Erik D. Stoops, Jeffrey L. Martin & Debbie L. Stone. Release date, January, 1995. Hardback and Paperback. Sterling Publishing Company, New York. Children's non-fiction, full-color, question and answer format. Third Book in Children's Nature Library Series.

Whales

Erik D. Stoops, Jeffrey L. Martin & Debbie L. Stone. Release date, March, 1995. Hardback and Paperback. Sterling Publishing Company, New York. Children's non-fiction, full-color, question and answer format. Fourth Book in Children's Nature Library Series.

Scorpions and Other Venomous Insects of the Desert

Erik D. Stoops & Jeffrey L. Martin. Release date, June, 1995. Golden West Publishing Company, Phoenix, Arizona. A user-friendly guide.

Alligators and Crocodiles

Erik D. Stoops & Debbie L. Stone. Release date, October, 1994. Sterling Publishing Company, New York. Children's non-fiction, full-color, question and answer format. Fifth Book in Children's Nature Library Series.

Wolves

Erik D. Stoops & Dagmar Fertl. Release date, December, 1996. Sterling Publishing Company, New York. Children's non-fiction, full-color, question and answer format. Sixth Book in Children's Nature Library Series.

Look for the Adventures of Dink the Skink Children's book series and animated CD Rom Stories coming out in 1997.

Internet Sites:

Zoo Net:
http://www.mindspring.com/~zoonet

Herp Link:
http://home.ptd.net/~herplink/index.html

Erik Stoops:
http://www.primenet.com/~dink

INDEX

WE WOULD LIKE TO THANK THE FOLLOWING PEOPLE FOR THEIR ENCOURAGEMENT AND PARTICIPATION:
NATIONAL ZOOLOGICAL PARK, OFFICE OF PUBLIC AFFAIRS, SUSAN BIGGS, SMITHSONIAN INSTITUTION,
TERRY CHRISTOPHER, TERRY ODEGAARD, CINCINNATI ZOO AND BOTANICAL GARDENS, ST. LOUIS ZOO,
BILL LUBACK'S REPTILES, INC., AMANDA JAKSHA, JESSIE COHEN, PAT TURCOTT, RODNEY FREEMAN,
DIANE E. FREEMAN, STEVEN CASTANEDA, CLYDE PEELINGS OF REPTILELAND, MICKEY OLSEN OF WILDLIFE
WORLD ZOO, SCOTTSDALE CHILDREN'S NATURE CENTER, DR. JEAN ARNOLD, ARIZONA GAME AND
FISH DEPARTMENT, ERIN DEAN OF THE UNITED STATES FISH AND WILDLIFE SERVICE,
BOB FAULKNER, DAVE PFEIFFER OF EDUCATION ON WHEELS FOR MAKING THIS PROJECT A REALITY,
DR. MARTY FELDMAN, SHERRIE STOOPS, ALESHA STOOPS, VICTORIA AND JESSICA EMERY.